# LIZARDS

## BY JOANNE MATTERN

**BENCHMARK BOOKS**

MARSHALL CAVENDISH
NEW YORK

Series Consultant:
James Doherty
General Curator
The Bronx Zoo, New York

With thanks to Samuel M. Lee, Senior Keeper, Department of Herpetology at The Bronx Zoo, New York
for his expert reading of this manuscript

Benchmark Books
Marshall Cavendish Corporation
99 White Plains Road
Tarrytown, NY 10591-9001
Website: www.marshallcavendish.us

Library of Congress Cataloging-in-Publication Data
Mattern, Joanne
Lizards / by Joanne Mattern.
p. cm – (Animals, animals)
Includes bibliographical references (p. ) and index.
1.Lizards–Juvenile literature. [1. Lizards.] I. Title. II. Series.
0-7614-1259-X

QL666.L2 M36 2001    597.95–dc21    00-052324

Cover photo: Visuals Unlimited, Inc.: © Joe McDonald

Illustration on page 10 by Daniel Roode

The photographs in this book are used by permission and through the courtesy of:
*Visuals Unlimited, Inc.*: © G and C Merker, 4, 7 (right), 26 (bottom), 27 (bottom), 40 (top);
John Gerlach: 6; Joe McDonald, 14 (bottom), 15, 27 (center), 32, 40 (bottom), 42; Ken Lucas, 19, 20;
Jeffrey Howe, 23; Jim Merli, 34, 38. *Animals Animals*: J.G. Acha, 7 (left), © Joe McDonald, 8, 26 (center);
Zig Leszczynski, 9, 11, 17, 24, 37; Lynn Stone, 14 (top); James Robinson, 22; Marian Bacon, 26 (top);
Michael Fogden, 27 (top); Stephen Dalton, 28; J. Frazier, 31; Robert Lubeck, 35;
Bruce Watkins (45). Michael Sewell/Visual Pursuit: 12. © Wolfgang Kaehler: 30.

Printed in China

3   5   6   4

# CONTENTS

# 1

# INTRODUCING LIZARDS

Lizards are members of a class of animals called reptiles. One of the oldest classes of animals, reptiles first appeared on Earth more than 250 million years ago. Other reptiles include snakes, turtles, crocodiles, and alligators.

All reptiles are alike in several ways. First, they are *cold-blooded*, which means they cannot control their body temperature. A reptile's temperature is the same as that of its surroundings, so lizards and all other reptiles are more active when the weather is warm, and sluggish when the temperature is cooler. In extreme temperatures, lizards must find a safe place to stay until the weather changes. If a lizard's body gets too

THE COMMON HOUSE GECKO—CALLED "CHICHAK" FOR THE SOUND OF ITS CALL—IS FOUND IN BALI AND THROUGHOUT SOUTHEAST ASIA. THE COLOR OF ITS SKIN CHANGES DEPENDING ON THE TEMPERATURE AND THE COLOR OF ITS SURROUNDINGS.

THIS ZEBRA-TAILED LIZARD IS RAISING ITS BODY OFF OF A HOT ROCK SO IT WON'T OVERHEAT.

hot or too cold, the animal may die.

Because a lizard is cold-blooded, it must work to maintain the temperature of its body. To keep warm, lizards often lie in the sun—a behavior that is called *basking*. The lizard will stay in the sun until its body warms up.

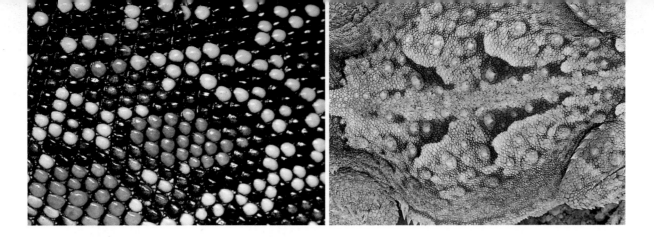

THE SCALES OF THE EYED LIZARD (LEFT) HAVE A BEADLIKE TEXTURE, WHILE THOSE OF THE HORNED LIZARD (RIGHT) ARE FLATTER AND LESS COLORFUL.

On the other hand, sometimes the sun can be too hot for a lizard. To keep its body from overheating, a lizard will seek shade—perhaps hiding under a rock or digging a hole in order to crawl underground.

Another thing that lizards have in common with other reptiles is skin made of scales. Although they may appear slimy, these scales are hard and dry. They protect the animal's body and help it to retain moisture.

As a lizard grows, its skin stays the same size. This means that the lizard periodically has to shed, or remove, its skin. The lizard's skin splits at the mouth and peels back. Sometimes lizards will rub their bodies against rocks or trees to work the skin off. When the lizard's old skin finally falls off, a new layer of scales is there underneath to replace it.

All lizards have lungs and breathe air, as humans do. A lizard breathes through a pair of nostrils just above its mouth. In addition to their noses, lizards smell with a special sense organ called the Jacobson's organ located on the roof of their mouth. A lizard flicks its tongue in the air to collect smells that then travel to the Jacobson's organ. In this way that lizards are able to sense if a *predator* or *prey* is nearby.

THIS COMMON TEGU LIZARD FLICKS OUT ITS TONGUE TO DETERMINE IF PREY IS NEARBY. THIS LIZARD'S FAVORITE MEAL IS A SMALL RODENT, BUT IT WILL ALSO EAT CHICKS, FISH, INSECTS AND OCCASIONALLY SOFT FRUITS.

A lizard's eyes and ears are located on either side of its head. The outer ear is just a hole in the skin, which is covered by a thin scale.

A lizard's body shape is very simple—a head, followed by a pair of legs, a long body, a second pair of legs and finally, the long tail. Lizards use their tail in many ways. It helps them to balance, to swim, or to grab tree branches as they climb. Some lizards even use their tail as a weapon or as a place to store fat.

THE POSITION OF THE FLAP-NECKED CHAMELEON'S EYES ALLOWS IT TO LOOK IN TWO DIRECTIONS AT ONCE.

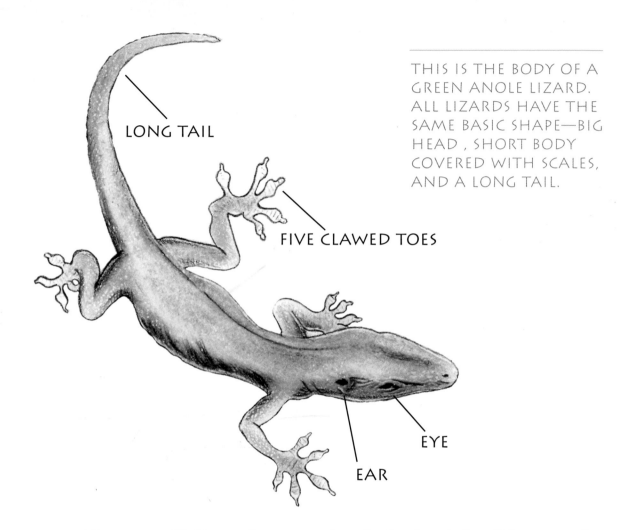

LONG TAIL

THIS IS THE BODY OF A GREEN ANOLE LIZARD. ALL LIZARDS HAVE THE SAME BASIC SHAPE—BIG HEAD , SHORT BODY COVERED WITH SCALES, AND A LONG TAIL.

FIVE CLAWED TOES

EYE

EAR

Almost all lizards can shed their tails. If a predator grabs the lizard by its tail, the lizard can twist certain muscles in the tail so it falls off. The lizard can do this because each of its tailbones has a small crack in it that allows it to break easily. While the predator is distracted by the wriggling tail, the rest of the lizard can escape. Later, the lizard will grow a new tail.

### THE GLASS LIZARD

THIS LEGLESS LIZARD IS OFTEN MISTAKEN FOR A SNAKE. ALTHOUGH IT HAS NO LEGS, IT DOES HAVE WELL-DEVELOPED EYELIDS AND EAR OPENINGS, TWO THINGS THAT SNAKES DO NOT HAVE. WHEN GRABBED BY A PREDATOR, THIS LIZARD'S TAIL SHATTERS INTO PIECES THAT CONTINUE TO SQUIRM. THIS CONFUSES THE PREDATOR AND GIVES THE GLASS LIZARD TIME TO ESCAPE.

Lizards come in many different sizes. The smallest lizard in the world is a type of gecko that lives in the British Virgin Islands. One of these geckos was only one-and-one-half inches (3.8 cm) long, including its tail. The largest lizard in the world is the Komodo dragon of Indonesia. These giants average seven-and-one-half feet (2.3 m) long and weigh about 130 pounds (59 kg). The largest Komodo dragon ever measured was more than ten feet (3 m) long and weighed over 300 pounds (135 kg).

12

Lizards can be found on every continent except Antarctica, where it is too cold for them to survive. Many lizards live in tropical rain forests. The hot and humid climate is just right for these animals who need warmth to live. Chameleons, geckos, and anoles all live in the rain forest. Because it is always warm and moist, the rain forest provides a wide variety of plants and insects throughout the year. This means that there is always something for lizards to eat.

Lizards can also be found in deserts and other hot dry regions. Many of these lizards are *nocturnal,* or active at night. The Gila monster's home is the desert in the southwestern United States and northeastern Mexico. During the day it is too hot for them to travel around the desert, so they stay in underground *burrows.* When the desert cools off at night, the Gila monster comes out to hunt for food.

Because of their mysterious habits people have long been fascinated by lizards. Ancient people thought that lizards had special powers and several cultures have included lizards as part of their mythology. Native peoples of the Amazon rain forest called the lizard the Master of Animals and Fish and believed it was a messenger of the gods. In Polynesia, the King of the Lizards was named Moko. He protected fishermen.

Several cultures also included lizards as part of their creation myths. Ancient Hawaiians believed in lizard gods who were ancestors of other animals. The Maori people of New Zealand believe a lizard pulled the first Maoris from the waters of creation. There is also a lizard hero in Australia's Aborigine culture. This lizard hero was the first one to separate men and women and also taught people the arts.

*The Mexican beaded lizard (top) is a close relative of the Gila monster. Both lizards live in the desert, have colorful scales that look like beads, and are venomous. The Mexican beaded lizard and the Gila monster are the only two venomous lizards in the world.*

WE CAN SEE WHY MONITOR LIZARDS HAVE INSPIRED FEAR IN HUMANS. WHITE-THROATED MONITORS LIKE THIS ONE CAN REACH FROM FOUR TO SIX FEET (1–2 M) IN LENGTH. THEY HAVE POWERFUL LEGS, SOMETIMES WALKING TWO TO THREE MILES (3–5 KM) PER DAY, AND WHIPLIKE TAILS AND SHARP TEETH THAT THEY WILL USE TO DEFEND THEMSELVES WHEN CORNERED.

Some lizards were viewed with fear. Native Americans who lived in the American Southwest believed that the Gila monster had venomous breath. They also thought a nursing mother would lose her milk if a Gila monster crossed her path, and that stepping on one would lead to a terrible illness. Since the Gila monster is *venomous*, it is easy to see the source of these superstitions!

In Asia, there are many superstitions about monitor lizards. These animals were often considered bad luck. In ancient Borneo, warriors sometimes painted monitor lizards on their shields to scare their enemies. If a monitor crossed the path of an advancing army, the battle would be postponed.

Today, we know that lizards are common animals with no magical powers—but they are still fascinating to us.

THE COMMON FLYING DRAGON OF SOUTHEAST ASIA DOES NOT REALLY FLY BUT GLIDES ON AIR CURRENTS. IT CAN TRAVEL MORE THAN 150 FEET (46 M) IN A SINGLE BOUND.

# 2
# LIZARD DEFENSES

Lizards, the largest group of reptiles, include about four thousand different *species*, or kinds, of lizard. All lizards share certain characteristics, but each species is somehow unique. Lizards have developed many different ways of defending themselves against predators.

The Komodo dragon is the most vicious lizard. Part of a group of lizards known as monitors, they can be found in the wild only on three islands in Indonesia. These animals are fierce predators that attack and eat both large and small animals. They have even been known to kill people. Their claws can rip a deer or wild pig to pieces, and their teeth and jaws are powerful enough to bring down a water buffalo. A Komodo dragon's saliva is full of germs so wounds from their bite often become infected and lead to the death of the victim. In addition to size and strength, the Komodo dragon's speed makes it an excellent hunter. They are able to move quickly both on land and in the water.

GREEN IGUANAS ARE SURVIVORS. THEY CAN FALL FROM A TREE TO THE GROUND AND WALK AWAY UNHARMED. THEY ARE EXCELLENT CLIMBERS AND SWIMMERS AND CAN DEFEND THEMSELVES WITH THEIR STRONG BITE, SHARP CLAWS, AND LONG TAIL.

THE KOMODO DRAGON IS THE WORLD'S LARGEST LIZARD.

The Gila monster, the only venomous lizard in the U.S., has black and pink patterned scales that warn other animals to leave it alone. Its Latin name is *Heloderma suspectum*, which means "frightful and suspicious." Gila monsters can grow to up to two feet (0.6 m) long. They store fat in their thick tails and can live off this fat if they cannot find food.

Green iguanas live in South and Central America, Trinidad and Tobago, and some islands in the West Indies. They have brightly colored skin, spines running down their back, and flaps of skin hanging around their throat. These spines and flaps help the iguana look bigger and more threatening than it really is—a feature that these animals have developed that protects them from predators.

Another lizard that uses its appearance to avoid predators is the chameleon. These animals can slowly change color when they are upset or frightened, or in response to changes in light or temperature. Changing color provides the lizard with *camouflage* and helps it hide from predators.

Chameleons have cone-shaped eyes that can move separately, allowing them to look at two things at the same time. There are about 130 species of chameleon. About sixty of these species live on the island of Madagascar, which is off the east coast of Africa. The others live in tropical climates in Africa and southern Asia.

THE GREEN ANOLE OF THE SOUTHEASTERN UNITED STATES IS SOMETIMES INCORRECTLY CALLED A CHAMELEON. ITS SKIN COLOR CAN CHANGE FROM GREEN TO BROWN DEPENDING ON ITS BODY TEMPERATURE, ENVIRONMENT, AND MOOD.

The gecko, one of the smallest lizards, also has un-usual body features. Its toes have special pads on the bottom that are covered with thousands of tiny bristles. These bristles stick to any surface, so that the gecko can climb straight up, and even walk upside-down! The many different types of geckos—over 750 species—live in warm places all over the world.

THANKS TO SPECIALIZED FOOT-PADS, THIS GECKO IS ABLE TO DEFY GRAVITY AND CLIMB A CEMENT WALL.

23

WHEN THE COLLARED
LIZARD RUNS FROM
DANGER ON ITS
HIND LEGS, IT LOOKS
LIKE A MINIATURE
*TYRANNOSARUS REX*
DINOSAUR.

24

The collared lizard of Mexico and the American southwest is named for the black bands around its neck. Although they only measure about eight to fourteen inches, they are strong and fierce. They will sometimes charge if challenged, but if they do choose to flee, they run off on all fours, gain speed, then lift themselves upright and run away on their hind legs.

# LIZARD SPECIES

Lizards are the largest living group of reptiles. Here are just six of the nearly four thousand species in this group. Measurements listed are for an adult male.

### Common water monitor
Malaysia
9 feet (3 m)

### Agama lizard
African savanna
10 inches (25 cm)

### Lesser earless
Southwestern
North America
5 inches (12 cm)

### Panther chameleon
Madagascar
12 inches (30 cm)

### Skunk gecko
Indonesia
9 inches (23 cm)

### Southern alligator lizard
Western United
States
up to 16 inches
(40 cm)

# 3
# A LIZARD'S DAY

When a lizard is not busy steering clear of predators, it is probably looking for its next meal. Lizards eat both plants and animals, and most do not limit their diet to any one thing.

Large *carnivores*, or meat-eaters, such as Komodo dragons, will eat any animal they can find—deer, wild pigs, cattle, and smaller dragons.

Gila monsters use *venom* to kill other lizards and small animals such as mice or baby

A MEDITERRANEAN CHAMELEON EXTENDS ITS TONGUE TO CATCH PREY.

animals such as baby birds. They do not inject the venom into their prey the way snakes do. Instead, the venom flows into the Gila monster's mouth from *glands* in its lower jaw. When the Gila monster bites its prey, the venom mixes into the wound. As the Gila monster chews, more venom flows into its prey's body. Gila monsters also eat reptile eggs and bird eggs.

THESE KOMODO DRAGONS ARE FEEDING ON A GOAT. ONCE A KOMODO ATTACKS AND KILLS ITS PREY, OTHER KOMODOS ARE OFTEN ATTRACTED BY THE SMELL AND ARRIVE TO JOIN THE FEAST.

Other, smaller carnivores eat insects, small animals, and other lizards. One such lizard is the thorny devil of Australia. This lizard, with a face resembling a miniature rhinoceros, dines only on ants. With its sticky tongue, this lizard can eat as many as forty-five ants per minute, snatching them up one at a time.

The *herbivores*, or plant-eaters, include the iguana, which eats many different kinds of plant material, like

THE THORNY DEVIL IS A SLOW-MOVING DESERT REPTILE THAT DOES NOT DRINK WATER THROUGH ITS MOUTH BUT RATHER ABSORBS IT THROUGH ITS SKIN.

SOME LIZARDS ARE OMNIVORES, OR ANIMALS THAT EAT BOTH PLANTS AND ANIMALS. THE BLUE-TONGUED SKINK (ABOVE) OF WESTERN AUSTRALIA IS OMNIVOROUS. SECRETIVE AND SOLITARY BY NATURE. THIS LIZARD HAS A LARGE HEAD, SHORT LEGS, A BROAD BODY, AND A SHORT, THICK TAIL. WHEN THREATENED, IT EXPANDS ITS RIBCAGE, OPENS ITS MOUTH WIDE, AND STICKS OUT ITS HUGE BLUE TONGUE.

leaves, fruit, and flowers. Although they don't have to chase and catch prey like carnivores do, herbivores still have to spend a lot of time looking for food.

How do lizards find food? Carnivores sometimes hide and wait for their food to come close enough to catch. Lizards that eat insects often wait near flowers and other places where insects like to gather. Herbivores have an easier time finding food. They just find a tree with tasty leaves or fruit and start eating!

Lizards are also prey for many different animals. A large lizard such as the Komodo dragon has few enemies, but smaller lizards may be eaten by birds, snakes, bears, coyotes, or raccoons.

Some lizards avoid predators by hunting after dark and spending the day hiding in underground burrows or under a stone or a tree. Lizards that are active during the day spend the nighttime in similar burrows or hiding places. Here they can sleep, stay warm, and keep safe.

Because lizards are cold-blooded, those that live in changeable climates have to *hibernate*, or sleep through the winter. To prepare for hibernation, lizards eat a lot of food. Some lizards, such as the Gila monster, can

store fat in their tails. When the weather gets cold, the lizard finds an underground burrow where it will be safe. It stays there until the weather is warm enough for the animal to survive outside.

Besides their need to keep warm, there is another reason that lizards hibernate during the cooler months—a lack of available food. Since the animals that lizards eat, such as insects and mice, are also unable to survive the winter, they either die or go into hibernation themselves when the temperature drops.

Lizards that live in tropical climates don't have to hibernate. The weather is warm enough for them to stay active all year, and there is always plenty of food for them to eat.

THE PLUMED BASILISK LIZARD
CAN BE FOUND IN THE RAIN
FOREST OF COSTA RICA.

# 4

# THE LIFE OF A LIZARD

**L**izards are solitary creatures, living most of their lives on their own. However, when mating season comes, males seek out the females.

Lizards use colors and other visual signals to find a mate. Males are usually much more brightly colored than females, and often have colorful fans, crests, or flaps of skin. During the mating season, males bob their heads and wave these fans around to attract the attention of a female. Once the male and female finish mating, they go their separate ways.

Most lizards hatch from eggs that are laid in damp places under rocks or in holes scraped in the ground. Most mother

THIS MADAGASCAR DAY GECKO HAS RECENTLY HATCHED AND IS ALREADY SHEDDING ITS FIRST SKIN.

A FEMALE BEARDED DRAGON LAYS HER EGGS IN A SHADED HOLE IN THE GROUND.

lizards do not care for the eggs or for the babies after they are born.

It takes from one to several months for lizard eggs to hatch. Usually, the warmer the nest site, the faster the eggs will hatch. Eggs that are laid in the late summer or the early fall must wait until spring to hatch.

Inside the egg, the baby lizard has a tiny *egg tooth* on the tip of its nose. It uses this tooth to break open the tough leathery eggshell. A few days after birth, the lizard sheds its skin and the tooth falls off.

A few species give birth to live young. These lizards grow in eggs inside their mother's body. Just before birth, the eggs hatch and live lizards are born.

The eggs of live–bearing lizards aren't tough or leathery. Instead, they are thin and transparent. This is

. . .

THE RECORD FOR THE LONGEST LIFE SPAN FOR A LIZARD BELONGS TO A SLOW WORM (A TYPE OF LIZARD WITHOUT LEGS) THAT LIVED IN A ZOO IN COPENHAGEN, DENMARK. THIS LIZARD WAS MORE THAN FIFTY-FOUR YEARS OLD WHEN IT DIED IN 1946.

. . .

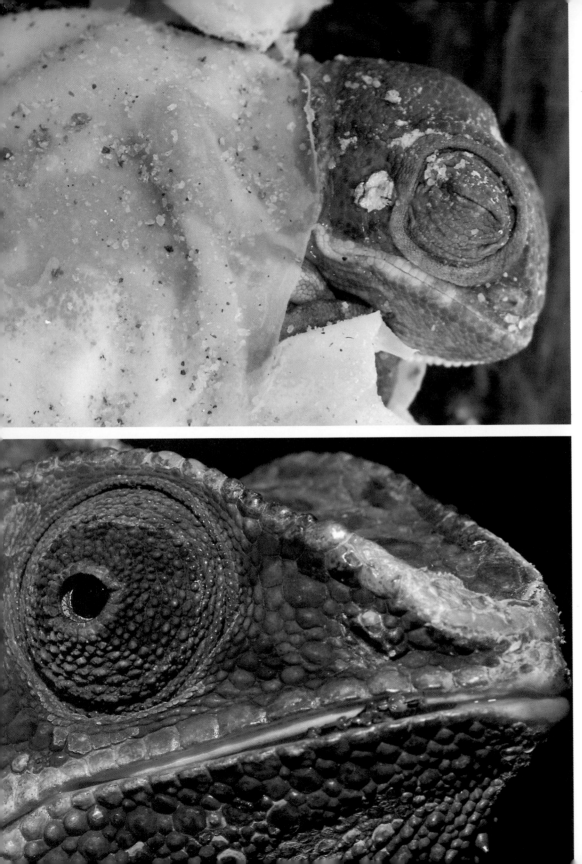

UPON HATCHING,
A CHAMELEON
CAN EASILY BE
IDENTIFIED. NOTICE
THE SIMILARITIES
BETWEEN THE BABY
AND THE ADULT.

because the eggs are inside the mother's body, so they don't need to be protected against predators or the loss of water.

Baby lizards look like tiny copies of their parents and are born knowing how to hunt and defend them-selves. Although it takes a few months to several years for the young lizards to reach adult size, they can take care of themselves right away.

Different lizards live for different lengths of time. Large lizards usually live longer than small lizards. Many small species live only one year before they are killed by predators or other dangers. On average, the life span of a lizard is between five and ten years.

# 5
# LIZARDS AND PEOPLE

Most of the time, lizards and people get along pretty well. Because lizards are usually small and shy, they can go about their business without getting in our way. Even dangerous lizards, such as the Komodo dragon and the Gila monster, rarely attack humans.

There are, however, some lizards that can cause trouble. Monitor lizards sometimes break into henhouses to kill chickens and eat eggs. Some fruit-eating lizards are poisoned or shot by farmers who want to protect their crops. But the threat to humans

TOKAY GECKOS ARE POPULAR PETS. IF YOU ARE CONSIDERING HAVING A LIZARD AS A PET, YOU SHOULD LEARN AS MUCH AS YOU CAN ABOUT ITS CARE BEFORE BRINGING IT HOME. TRY TO PURCHASE ONE THAT WAS BORN IN CAPTIVITY SINCE TAKING A LIZARD OUT OF ITS NATURAL HABITAT WILL PUT ITS LIFE AT RISK.

is minor in comparison to the problems we create for lizards. People threaten lizards in several ways.

The biggest threat to lizards is the destruction of their *habitats,* or the places where they live. Today, many rain forests are being cut down to supply land for houses, farms, and roads, and to use the wood for fuel. When rain forests disappear, the animals that live there lose their homes.

Rain forests aren't the only habitats that are in danger. Swamps and marshes are often drained of their water to provide land for buildings. People are also finding ways to live in the desert, which limits the room for animals.

Loss of habitat has made some lizards *endangered* species. One of these endangered animals is the Komodo dragon. Because this lizard only lives in one place in the world, it could disappear completely if its habitat were changed or destroyed.

In some parts of the world, people hunt lizards for food. People in Asia and Africa eat monitor lizards, and Central and South Americans sometimes eat iguanas.

In the past, many lizards were killed for their skins. People made belts and other items of clothing from lizard skins. It is now against the law to sell lizard skins in many parts of the world. This law has helped some lizard populations survive.

Another danger to lizards is the pet trade. Many people keep iguanas, chameleons, geckos, anoles, and other lizards as pets. Sometimes lizards are taken out of the wild to be sold as pets, which means there are fewer lizards in the wild. This practice can also introduce diseases into the pet population. These diseases can kill many lizards and reduce the numbers of these animals.

The good news is that there are people who are helping to protect lizards. Organizations have been formed to try to save rare lizards by protecting habitat, educating the public about their national treasures, and by breeding lizards in captivity. These captive-bred lizards may then be released back into the wild to create the next generation.

THE FATE OF THE WORLD'S FEW THOUSAND REMAINING KOMODO DRAGONS IS NOW IN HUMAN HANDS.

**basking:** to lie in the sun to stay warm.

**burrow:** a tunnel or hole in the ground.

**camouflage:** body coloring that makes an animal hard to see.

**carnivore:** an animal that eats meat.

**cold-blooded:** an animal whose body is the same temperature as its surroundings.

**egg tooth:** a special tooth on the tip of a lizard's nose that it uses to break out of the egg.

**endangered:** threatened

**gland:** an organ in the body that produces a chemical.

**habitat:** the preferred place for an animal species to live.

**herbivore:** an animal that eats plants.

**hibernate:** to become inactive during cold weather.

**nocturnal:** active at night.

**predator:** an animal that hunts other animals for food.

**prey:** an animal that is hunted by another animal.

**species:** a group of animals that are all of the same kind.

**venom:** a poisonous substance made in the body of an animal.

## BOOKS

Fichter, George S. *Snakes and Lizards.* Racine, WI: Western Publishing Co., NY: Golden, 1993.

Gravelle, Karen. *Lizards.* New York: Franklin Watts, 1991.

Miller, Sara Swan. *Snakes and Lizards: What They Have in Common.* New York: Franklin Watts, 2000.

Roberts, M.L. *World's Weirdest Reptiles.* Mahwah, NJ: Watermill Press, 1994.

Smith, Trevor. *Amazing Lizards.* New York: Knopf, 1990.

## WEBSITES

Discovery.com
http://www.discovery.com/exp/lizards/world.html

Giant Lizards
http://unmuseum.mus.pa.us/bigliz.htm

Sedgwick County Zoo
http://www.scz.org/animals

The Basking Spot
http://www.baskingspot.com

NetVet—Reptiles
http://netvet.wustl.edu/reptiles.htm

## ABOUT THE AUTHOR

**Joanne Mattern** has always loved animals, both wild and tame. She is the author of more than 125 books for young people, including Sharks in the Animals Animals series. She lives with her husband, daughter, two cats, and a dog in New York State.

# INDEX

Page numbers for illustrations are in **boldface.**